D1522377

Swimming
Giants

by Monica Hughes

Consultant: Luis M. Chiappe, Ph.D.
Director of the Dinosaur Institute
Natural History Museum of Los Angeles County

BEARPORT
PUBLISHING

NEW YORK, NEW YORK

Credits

Cover, Title Page, 14–15, 16–17, 24: Luis Rey; 4–5: John Alston; 5, 6, 12–13, 19, 20–21, 23B: Simon Mendez; 7, 8, 9, 10–11, 18, 22, 23M, 23T: Shutterstock.

Every effort has been made by ticktock Entertainment Ltd. to trace copyright holders. We apologize in advance for any omissions. We would be pleased to insert the appropriate acknowledgments in any subsequent edition of this publication.

Library of Congress Cataloging-in-Publication Data

Hughes, Monica.
 Swimming giants / by Monica Hughes.
     p. cm. — (I love reading. Dino world!)
 Includes bibliographical references and index.
 ISBN-13: 978-1-59716-542-6 (library binding)
 ISBN-10: 1-59716-542-5 (library binding)
 1. Marine reptiles, Fossil—Juvenile literature. 2. Marine animals, Fossil—Juvenile literature. 3. Paleontology—Juvenile literature. I. Title.

 QE861.5.H846 2008
 567.9'37—dc22

                                    2007017958

Contents

Swimming giants

Many animals lived at the same time as dinosaurs.

Some of these animals lived in water.

Ceresiosaurus
(ser-*ree*-see-oh-SOR-uhss)

Many of them had very sharp teeth.

They used their teeth to catch fish and other animals.

Kronosaurus
(*kroh*-noh-SOR-uhss)

This swimmer grew to about 30 feet (9 m) long.

It was about the size of a power boat.

Its teeth were as big as bananas.

Kronosaurus ate **squid** and **octopuses**.

squid

octopus

Placodus
(PLAK-oh-duhss)

Placodus was about 7 feet (2 m) long.

It was as big as some sea lions.

sea lion

Placodus walked on the ocean floor.

It dug up shellfish with its long front teeth.

Elasmosaurus
(eh-*lazz*-moh-SOR-uhss)

Elasmosaurus was longer than a school bus.

It was up to 46 feet (14 m) long from head to tail.

Its neck was longer than the rest of its body.

Its legs were shaped like **paddles**.

They helped the animal swim slowly through the water.

Nothosaurus
(*noth*-oh-SOR-uhss)

Nothosaurus grew to about 10 feet (3 m) long.

It was about as big as some **alligators**.

Nothosaurus could walk on land like a seal.

However, it spent most of its time in the sea.

It had **webbed** feet to help it swim.

webbed feet

Cryptoclidus
(*krip*-toh-KLYE-duhss)

Part of *Cryptoclidus* looked like a snake.

Part of it looked like a turtle.

Cryptoclidus had more than 100 long, scary teeth.

It used its teeth to chomp on fish and squid.

Ichthyosaurus
(*ik*-thee-oh-SOR-uhss)

Ichthyosaurus is a long name that means "fish-lizard."

This animal could swim as fast as 25 miles per hour (40 kph).

The best human swimmers can only swim about 5 miles per hour (8 kph).

Ichthyosaurus ate mostly fish and squid.

Shonisaurus
(*shon*-ee-SOR-uhss)

Shonisaurus was about as long as two elephants.

It was shaped like a whale.

Shonisaurus lived in groups in the ocean.

It swam well, even in deep water.

Tylosaurus

(*tye*-loh-SOR-uhss)

Tylosaurus was a huge ocean lizard.

It was a little longer than *Shonisaurus*.

Tylosaurus grew to about 30 feet (9 m) long.

It ate fish and other sea animals.

Glossary

alligators (AL-i-*gay*-tuhrz) large reptiles with strong jaws and sharp teeth

octopuses (OK-tuh-*puhss*-iz) sea animals that have a soft body and eight arms

paddles (*PAD*-uhlz)
flat blades used to move
and steer small boats

squid (SKWID)
long, soft sea animals
that have ten arms

webbed (WEBD)
having toes
connected by skin

23

Index

Read More

Lessem, Don. *Sea Giants of Dinosaur Time.* Minneapolis, MN: Lerner Publications (2005).

Taylor, Barbara. *Oxford First Book of Dinosaurs.* New York: Oxford University Press (2001).

Learn More Online

To learn more about the world of dinosaurs, visit
www.bearportpublishing.com/ILoveReading